How to Beat Obamacare

Edward A. Lyon, JD CTC
Michael J. McCormick, CPA, CTC
Thomas J. Quigley, Jr.
Christy A. Quigley

ClaimLinx, LLC
10260 Alliance Road, Suite 130
Cincinnati OH 45242
www.claimlinx.com

The Pocket Guide to Obamacare
Copyright © 2013 by Lucror, LLC

Contents

Introduction

Back in 2010, President Obama signed the "Patient Protection and Affordable Care Act" and companion "Health Care and Education Reconciliation Act of 2010." Together, those two acts, better known by Republicans and Democrats alike as "Obamacare," represent the biggest change in how we finance healthcare since Medicare was created in 1965. They also include some of the most significant tax changes in a generation.

In 2012, the U.S. Supreme Court ruled that the Act's controversial "individual mandate" was a constitutional exercise of the government's power to tax. The Court's decision dashed the hopes of those who wanted to see it eliminated the "easy" way. And despite the decision, Obamacare remains an intensely political issue. Republican candidate Mitt Romney made the law a centerpiece of his 2012 presidential campaign, vowing to undo it on his first day in office. And despite his loss, Republicans in the House of Representatives continue to pass votes opposing the law.

Polls show that even today, Americans are confused and concerned. (One poll, taken in August 2013, revealed that four out of ten believed it was repealed, overturned, or were unsure if it was still law. *Four out of ten!*) Even Americans who understand that Obamacare is still law generally don't know just what it does, and they don't know how much it's going to cost.

We're not here to debate the merits of the law – it's going to take a long time before historians can make that call. But we *can* help by outlining what the law means for you, for your healthcare, and for your taxes.

This book is called "How to Beat Obamacare" for a reason. We're not here to give you a comprehensive guide to all things Obamacare. (There's no shortage of those guides already available for *that*.) Instead, we want to briefly cover the most important parts of the law and give you a framework for making smart choices in the new healthcare environment. So if you have questions, just ask, we'll be glad to help you work through them!

It's also worth noting that, whenever you may be reading these words, we're *writing* them in the first week of October, 2013. Insurance exchanges have just begun enrolling consumers (but not on small-business exchanges, or *en espanol*). The Obama administration has announced plans to delay the individual mandate until 2015. And Republicans in Congress are *still* working to repeal the whole thing. (More about all of those issues later.) Not a week passes without major news about implementing the law. There's still much to learn about Obamacare, and much that we simply can't know yet. So we'll all have to keep our eyes open and our wits about us as events unfold.

How the Law Works

Let's start by walking through the law's main provisions. First we'll talk about what changes when, because the law's implementation is spread out over several years. Then we'll talk about the specific changes in more detail.

Many Americans look at news reports talking about "upcoming Obamacare changes" and think it's something from the future. But few of us realize how much Obamacare has *already* affected Americans, and how much it's already woven into the fabric of our healthcare system. Take a look at just a few of the ways Obamacare has already changed how you or someone you know gets their care:

- 6.6 million young adults, including 3.1 million who were previously uninsured, now have coverage through the provisions letting them stay on their parents' plans until age 26.

- 17 million children cannot be denied coverage because of pre-existing conditions.

- 15 million Americans can no longer be dropped by their insurance company for unintentional mistakes in their insurance applications.

- 6.1 million seniors have saved over $5.7 billion on prescription drugs. In 2012 alone, over 3.5 million seniors and people with disabilities who reached the Medicare Part D "donut hole" received more than $2.5 billion in discounts, averaging $706 per beneficiary.

- The percentage of doctors adopting electronic health records increased from 48% in 2009 to 72% in 2012.

Keep all of that in mind as you read the next few pages. Obamacare is already here, ready or not!

2010 Changes

Tax Provisions	Healthcare Provisions
Certain small businesses with up to 25 employees get credit of up to 35% of the cost of providing employee health benefits	Cannot deny children coverage for pre-existing conditions
	No more lifetime limits on coverage
10% excise tax applies on indoor tanning services using certain UV lights	Children can remain on parents' plans until age 26
	Medicare Part D "donut hole" rebate

The first changes went into effect pretty much as soon as the law passed. On the tax side, small businesses with up to 25 employees, each earning $50,000/year or less, qualified for a new tax credit of up to 35% of the cost of providing health benefits to their employees. We'll talk more about that credit shortly. Oh, and who can overlook the new 10% excise tax on indoor tanning services that use certain ultraviolet lights? That rule took effect on July 1, just as outdoor tanning season went into full swing. (Yes, we want to *prevent* health problems that affect us, rather than just *treating* them . . . but, really?)

On the healthcare side, starting in 2010, insurance companies no longer could deny coverage to children for pre-existing conditions. They can't set lifetime limits on plan coverage. And they have to let children stay on their parents' plans through age 26. Insurance companies actually stepped up to the plate early on this rule – they loved charging new premium dollars for healthy, young-adult customers who aren't likely to cost them much anyway.

Finally, Medicare Part D recipients who enter the so-called "donut hole" will get rebates and discounts on prescription drug coverage. (The "donut hole" is a gap in prescription coverage where the government pays nothing and beneficiaries pay the full cost of drugs themselves.)

2011 Changes

Tax Provisions	Healthcare Provisions
Penalty tax for Health Savings Account/Medical Savings Account distributions doubles	Medicare Part D "donut hole" discount

2011 wasn't an especially consequential year for Obamacare. On the tax side, starting in 2011, the penalty tax on Health

Savings Account withdrawals not used for health care expenses doubled from 10% to 20%. And on the healthcare side, Medicare Part D recipients entering the "donut hole" began qualifying for discounts rather than rebates on their prescription drugs.

2012 Changes

Tax Provisions	Healthcare Provisions
W2 reporting requirements apply for employers with 250+ employees	Medical Loss Ratio rules require carriers to issue rebates if losses fall below 85% of premiums.

2012 wasn't an especially busy year for Obamacare either, if you don't count the attorneys busy challenging or defending it in various courts! On the tax side, starting for tax year 2012, employers with 250 or more employees must start reporting the aggregate value of the health coverage they provide their employees on Form W2. This reporting is for informational purposes only and does not add anything to anyone's taxable income.

On the insurance side, special new "Medical Loss Ratio" limits apply to insurers. This new rule states that "large" group health plans (defined differently by various by states as 50+ or 100+ for 2012-2015, but fixed at 100+ from 2016 on) must apply at least 85% of all premiums towards claims and quality improvement costs. Otherwise, they must rebate the difference to the policyholder. Individual and smaller plans must apply at least 80% of premiums towards claims and quality improvement.

2013 Changes

Tax Provisions	Healthcare Provisions
7.5% floor for deducting medical and dental expenses climbs to 10% (for taxpayers age 65 or older, floor stays at 7.5% until 2016).	Limit health insurer's executive compensation deduction to $500,000
Healthcare FSA contributions capped at $2,500/year.	
Medicare surtax on earned income above $200,000 (individuals) or $250,000 (joint filers)	
Medicare tax on "investment income"	

2013 is a big year for tax changes:

- Up until 2013, medical and dental expenses were deductible if they exceeded 7.5% of your adjusted gross income (AGI). Unless, of course, you're subject to Alternative Minimum Tax (AMT), in which case they have to exceed 10% of your AGI. Starting in 2013, that floor rose to 10% of AGI for everyone. *Unless* you or your spouse are 65 or older – in which case it stays at 7.5% of

AGI until 2016. Unless, of course, you're 65 *and* subject to AMT. Are we all clear here?

- If you participate in a healthcare flexible spending account at work, your contributions will be capped at $2,500/year, with no contributions for over-the-counter medications.

- If your earned income is above $200,000 – or $250,000 if you file jointly – you'll pay an extra 0.9% Medicare tax on earned income above those amounts. Given the new marginal tax rates in 2013 "fiscal cliff" legislation, that extra Medicare tax could help push your actual marginal rate well above 40%.

- Finally, you'll pay a 3.8% "Unearned Income Medicare Contribution" on investment income if your AGI is above those same thresholds. "Investment income" is defined as interest, dividends, capital gains, rents, royalties, and annuities. We'll talk a bit later about strategies for avoiding this new tax.

This new Medicare tax might not seem like a big deal, especially if your income isn't high enough that you'll actually pay it. Hey, it's just 3.8%, right? How bad can that be? Well, leaving aside the fact that a new tax still hurts, this is the first time investment income has ever been subject to Medicare tax. And lots of commentators fear it's just the proverbial camel's nose "under the tent" for even higher taxes. After all, it's a lot easier for legislators to go from 3.8% to 5.8% than it is to go from 0 to 3.8%. So we'll be paying lots of attention to this provision.

On the healthcare side, starting in 2013, the new law limits health insurance company deductions for executive compensation to $500,000 per person, as opposed to the regular $1 million for other businesses. It doesn't *stop* insurance companies from paying their top executives more than half a million – it just stops them from deducting anything over that amount on their *own* tax returns.

2014 Changes

Tax Provisions	Healthcare Provisions
Most individuals must maintain "minimum essential coverage" or face penalties	Insurance companies cannot deny adults coverage for pre-existing conditions
	Plans can no longer set annual limits on coverage
Businesses with >50 employees must offer health coverage or pay penalty of $2,000/employee	
	Medicaid expands to cover all Americans with income up to 138% of poverty line
	State-run insurance "exchanges" begin offering coverage to individuals and small businesses

2014 brings the most controversial changes. Specifically, this is the year when the "individual mandate" and "employer mandate" were both scheduled to begin:

- Most individuals who aren't covered through their employer will have to maintain "minimum essential coverage" or pay individual penalties. This is the so-called "individual mandate" you've heard so much about. We'll talk about that more in a bit, too.

- Employers with more than 50 employees *must* offer health benefits or pay a penalty of up to $2,000 per employee. If they offer coverage that doesn't meet minimum standards, the penalty could jump to $3,000. (The Obama administration has since postponed this requirement to 20*15*.) We'll talk about this in more detail in a bit.

2014 is also the year when the biggest insurance and healthcare changes go into effect. Specifically:

- Insurance companies can't deny coverage to *anyone* for pre-existing conditions. (Remember, starting back in 2010 they could no longer deny coverage to *children* for pre-existing conditions.)

- Plans can't set *annual* limits on coverage. (Remember, the ban on *lifetime* limits took effect in 2010.)

- States can choose (or *not* choose) to expand Medicaid eligibility to non-elderly, non-pregnant individuals with incomes up to 138% of the federal poverty level. For 2014-2016, the federal government will pick up 100% of those costs.

- The law requires states to establish insurance "exchanges," or join a federal exchange, where individuals and small businesses can comparison-shop for coverage. We'll talk about those "exchanges" in more detail shortly.

- All health insurance plans must provide coverage for "essential benefits," in categories such as maternity care, substance abuse services, mental and behavioral health services, and prescription drugs. The trade association America's Health Insurance Plans, which represents 1,300 health insurance companies, estimates that these "essential benefit" provisions may raise premiums as much as 33% in states that currently allow more stripped-down plans.

2018 Changes

Tax Provisions	Healthcare Provisions
Impose 40% excise tax on "Cadillac plans" costing above $10,200 (singles) or $27,500 (families)	

The law doesn't specify any significant new changes in years 2015-2017. But finally, in 2018, it imposes a 40% excise tax on "Cadillac plans" costing more than $10,200 per year for singles or $27,500 per year for families. The goal here is simply to rein in costs on these most-expensive plans. (And they really *are* pretty pricey – the average American family doesn't pay nearly that much for its *mortgage*.)

There's evidence to suggest this provision is already working – employers who are likely to be affected by the tax have begun cutting back on some of the most generous plans by raising deductibles, co-pays, prescriptions, and the like. But this provision doesn't take actual effect until 2018 – which some commentators think means it won't ever take effect at all.

Three Requirements

1. Must pay at least 50% of premium
2. Under 25 employees
3. Under $50,000 average wage

Now let's talk about specific provisions in more detail. We'll start with the new tax credits for small employers, which went into effect all the way back in 2010.

To qualify for the credit, you have to pay at least 50% of the "employee-only" premium amount for your employees' coverage. You can't have more than 24 "full-time equivalent" employees, or FTEs. Your average wage can't be more than $50,000 per year. Oh, and you can't claim the credit for any premium you pay on your *own* behalf.

Figure 2: Phaseout of the Credit for Small Businesses as a Percentage of Employer Contributions to Premiums, for 2010 to 2013

Number of FTEs	Average wage					
	$25,000 and less	$30,000	$35,000	$40,000	$45,000	$50,000
10 and fewer	35%	28%	21%	14%	7%	0%
11	33%	26%	19%	12%	5%	0%
12	30%	23%	16%	9%	2%	0%
13	28%	21%	14%	7%	0%	0%
14	26%	19%	12%	5%	0%	0%
15	23%	16%	9%	2%	0%	0%
16	21%	14%	7%	0%	0%	0%
17	19%	12%	5%	0%	0%	0%
18	16%	9%	2%	0%	0%	0%
19	14%	7%	0%	0%	0%	0%
20	12%	5%	0%	0%	0%	0%
21	9%	2%	0%	0%	0%	0%
22	7%	0%	0%	0%	0%	0%
23	5%	0%	0%	0%	0%	0%
24	2%	0%	0%	0%	0%	0%
25	0%	0%	0%	0%	0%	0%

For 2010 through 2013, the maximum credit is 35% of the amount of premium you pay. It goes down if you have more than 10 employees or average wages of more than $25,000.

Starting in 2014, the maximum credit goes up to 50% of premiums paid. If the credit is more than the business owes, you can carry it back against previous taxes you paid, or carry it forward to offset future taxes.

This all sounds great, right? The reality is, for 2010, just 170,000 employers across the country claimed any credit at all, and only 28,100 claimed the full credit. The fact is, small employers with low payrolls just can't afford to buy insurance for their employees. And the credit isn't enough to encourage them to start. Spending a buck on new benefits to save 35 cents in tax is hardly a winning proposition, especially for struggling small businesses.

The Individual Mandate

"Individual Mandate"	
Year	**Penalty**
2014	$95/adult up to 1.0% of income
2015	$325/adult up to 2.0% of income
2016+	$695/adult up to 2.5% of income

The most controversial part of the law is the "individual mandate." The law says that by 2014, all Americans have to maintain "minimum essential coverage" or face a penalty.

That mandate is a pretty big step. The government has never required us to buy commercial products or services before. If you drive a car, most states mandate you buy car insurance – but nobody says you *have* to drive a car in the first place. If you practice a profession, your state's licensing board may require you to carry malpractice insurance – but nobody says you *have* to practice that profession in the first place.

That requirement was so controversial that it became the focus of *National Federation of Independent Business v. Sebelius*, the

Supreme Court's Obamacare decision. The court eventually ruled that while the individual mandate was *not* a constitutional exercise of the Constitution's Commerce Clause, it *was* a constitutional exercise of the government's power to tax.

Now that we understand why the individual mandate is so controversial, let's take a look at the actual bite. The penalty starts at $95 per adult or $47.50 per child, up to a maximum of $285 per family or 1% of income in 2014. It rises to $695 per adult or $347.50 per child, up to a maximum of $2,085 per family or 2.5% of income in 2016. After 2016, those dollar amounts are indexed for inflation. That's it.

Now, there are lots of ways you can get that essential coverage. You can get it from your employer. You can get it from your spouse's employer. You can buy it on your own in the individual marketplace or on your state's exchange. You can get it through Medicare, Medicaid, or your state's Children's Health Insurance program (CHIP). You can get it through Tricare (active-duty military personnel and veterans). The law doesn't really care *where* your coverage comes from as long as you have it.

Section 5000(A)(f) of the Internal Revenue Code defines employer-sponsored "minimum essential coverage" to mean: "a group health plan or group health insurance coverage offered by an employer to the employee which is [either a government-sponsored plan] or 'any other plan or coverage offered in the small or large group market within a State.'" So, pretty much any legally-available coverage will satisfy the requirement.

Every year, your insurance company will send you and the IRS a form confirming you have coverage. You'll get to attach your copy of the form to your income-tax return, which will surely become a delightful exercise in government red tape.

And there are plenty of exceptions to the new mandate:

- If your taxable income is under the federal poverty line, or the cost of coverage is more than 8% of your household income, you don't have to pay the penalty. For purposes of this rule, "household income" is defined as total income in excess of the filing threshold, which is $10,000 for an individual and $20,000 for a family in 2013.

- This provision means a lot of people will escape penalties under the law – especially older people. Remember, the older you get, the higher your premiums go. If you're 35 years old, and coverage costs $300 per month, you're required to buy so long as your income is $45,000 (because the $3,600 premium is just 8% of your $45,000 income). If you're 55 years old, that same coverage may cost $600 per month. In that case, you're required to buy only if your income tops $90,000 per year.

- If your taxable income is less than four times the federal poverty limit, you may qualify for subsidies to help pay for your coverage. (We'll discuss these subsidies in more detail a little later in the book.)

- The penalty is pro-rated by the number of months you go without coverage – so if you're without coverage for just half a year, you pay just half the penalty.

- There's no penalty for a gap in coverage that lasts less than three months.

- Finally, the penalty can't be greater than the national average premium for "Bronze" coverage in an exchange, which we'll discuss in a bit.

But here's the weirdest thing about the penalty – and perhaps the weirdest part about the entire Obamacare law. *There's no real way for the government to <u>enforce</u> that penalty.*

Section 1501(g)(2) of the Affordable Care Act specifically states that the IRS can't subject you to any criminal prosecution or penalty for failing to pay the fine. It also says the IRS can't file liens or levy assets to enforce it.

And here's what the Congressional Joint Committee on Taxation had to say in their explanation of the bill:

> *"The penalty is assessed through the Code and accounted for as an additional amount of Federal tax owed. However, it is not subject to the enforcement provisions of subtitle F of the Code. The use of liens and seizures otherwise authorized for collection of taxes does not apply to the collection of this penalty. Non-compliance with the personal responsibility requirement to have health coverage is not subject to criminal or civil penalties under the Code and interest does not accrue for failure to pay such assessments in a timely manner."*

So, right now, it looks like the worst the IRS can do is withhold your future tax refunds. Other than that, there's nothing they're legally authorized to do to collect. No interest. No liens. No levies. No jail time. *Nada.*

It will be interesting to see how hard the IRS works to enforce a penalty Congress says it's not allowed to enforce! Who knows how many Americans will actually pay if there's no real consequence for not doing it?

Insurance Exchanges

Insurance "Exchanges"

- State or federal
- Online comparison
- Guaranteed issue

Now let's walk through the new insurance "exchanges" and see how they're supposed to work. The law requires them to start offering coverage on January 1, 2014; however, they actually began enrolling consumers on October 1, 2013.

The goal of the exchanges is to establish a more organized and competitive market where consumers can learn about their options and compare standardized plans. Exchanges are intended mainly for those who don't have employer-based coverage, those whose income is too high for Medicaid, and small employers looking to buy coverage for their employees.

Obamacare lets states establish their own exchanges, partner with the federal government to run their exchange, merge their exchanges with other states, or default into a federal "mega-exchange." As of this writing, 16 states and the District of Columbia have announced they would establish their own exchange, 7 announced plans for a partnership exchange, and 27 planned to default to the federal exchange:

- AL – Federal
- AK – Federal
- AZ – Federal
- AR -- Partnership
- CA -- State
- CO -- State
- CT -- State
- DC -- State
- DE -- State
- FL – Federal
- GA -- Federal
- HI -- State
- ID -- Federal
- IL -- Partnership
- IN -- Federal
- IA -- Partnership
- KS -- Federal
- KY -- State
- LA -- Federal
- ME -- Federal
- MD -- State
- MA -- State
- MI -- Partnership
- MN -- State
- MI -- Federal
- MO -- Federal
- MT -- Federal
- NE -- Federal
- NV -- State
- NH -- Federal
- NJ -- Federal
- NM -- State
- NY -- State
- NC -- Partnership
- ND -- Federal
- OH -- Federal
- OK -- Federal
- OR -- State
- PA -- Federal
- RI -- State
- SC -- Federal
- SD -- Federal
- TN -- Federal
- TX -- Federal
- UT -- State
- VT -- State
- VA -- Federal
- WA -- State
- WV -- Partnership
- WI -- Federal
- WY -- Federal

The "exchange" itself can be a government agency or a nonprofit organization. Its main function will be to provide a website where consumers can compare the different plans. The idea here is that making it easier for consumers to compare plans will force insurance companies to be more competitive. If you've ever bought plane tickets on a site like Travelocity or Expedia, that lays out different airlines' pricing and schedules side-by-side, you'll "get" the idea.

The law also authorizes insurance exchanges to hire and train "navigators" to help you through the maze of choices. (Unfortunately, it doesn't make money available to actually *pay* the navigators until 2014, after the first rush of applications.) And those navigators have a real challenge ahead of them. Many of the people who are currently uninsured have a hard time with English, or no internet access. Thousands more have never bought health insurance before. They have no clue what "copays" or "deductibles" are. Many won't be equipped to calculate subsidies on their own.

The numbers alone here are daunting. Colorado anticipates enrolling 150,000 people in their exchange – 800 per day, seven days per week – during the first six-month enrollment period running from October 1, 2013 through March, 2014. California expects to certify 21,000 navigators. No wonder some skeptics expect the exchanges to crash and burn!

You might think hiring "navigators" to walk people through the exchange process would be noncontroversial. Think again. It turns out some states have introduced or passed legislation imposing certification and licensing requirements, regulating what they can do on consumers' behalf, or restricting them from giving advice about plans and benefits. Insurance brokers have also joined the fight, arguing the new navigators won't have the necessary expertise to help consumers make the right choices. So this is yet another area where we'll just have to wait and see what happens.

Now let's take a look at the plans themselves.

Exchange Plans

Plan	Target Benefit
Bronze	60%
Silver	70%
Gold	80%
Platinum	90%

The insurance exchanges will offer four levels of coverage: bronze, silver, gold, and platinum. There will also be a bare-bones "catastrophic-only" plan for those under age 30.

- The bronze plan is designed to cover 60% of the average insured's healthcare costs.

- The silver plan is designed to cover 70%.

- The gold plan is designed to cover 80%.

- Finally, the platinum plan is designed to cover 90%.

Each level will offer different premiums, copays, deductibles, and other out-of-pocket expenses. The law limits out-of-pocket expenses for any of these plans to no more than $6,350 for individuals and $12,700 for families.

- Premiums will vary by age, just like they do now. However, the premium difference between younger and older insureds will be less than before Obamacare. (Remember, part of the law's overall purpose is to draw more young, healthy people into the overall system to help subsidize older insured who use more healthcare services.)

- All other factors being equal, men and women will pay the same premium.

- If you smoke, now might be a good time to quit – premiums will be up to 50% higher for smokers.

- Remember, starting in 2014, insurance companies can't turn you down for pre-existing conditions. If you apply for coverage, you *will* qualify.

As of this writing, federal officials have just revealed the actual premiums to be offered through the exchanges. Generally, it looks like young, healthy insureds will pay more than they currently do, while older, sicker insureds will pay less. Also in September, 2013, the Kaiser Family Foundation released a study titled "An Early Look at Premiums and Insurer Participation in Health Insurance Marketplaces, 2014," examining the first premiums from the 17 states and District of Columbia that had already made data publicly available. That report found that premiums would be lower than the Congressional Budget Office originally expected and suggested that "the cost of coverage for consumers and the federal budgetary cost for tax credits will be lower than anticipated."

We also don't know what will happen with those premiums over time. We can certainly expect them to go *up*, of course. But that's never been in doubt. The real question is whether they'll increase faster or slower than they would have without Obamacare.

But the actual premiums may be less important than a lot of people worry they might be. That's because many people who end up buying coverage on an exchange will qualify for federal subsidies. (A recent Kaiser Family Foundation study estimates that 48% of Americans will qualify for subsidies.) So the real question may not be "how much is my premium"? The real question may be "how much is my *subsidized* premium based on my income"? We'll discuss that next.

Premium Subsidies

Two requirements:

1. Household income < 400% poverty level
2. Premium > 9.5% of "household income"

Federal subsidies are the "flip side" of the insurance exchanges. It doesn't do much good for Obamacare to lay out standardized plans for you to pick and choose from, or even guarantee you'll qualify for coverage, if you just plain can't *afford* it. So the law offers subsidies to help afford the newly required coverage.

You'll qualify for subsidies if you meet TWO conditions:

- First, your "household income" is below 400% of the federal poverty level, or "FPL." For 2013, that's $23,550 for a family of four, which makes subsidies available for incomes up to $94,200. "Household income" includes income from you, your spouse, and any dependents.

- Second, if you have an employer who offers coverage, your share of the premium has to be more than 9.5% of your household income. So, if your household income is $50,000, and your premium is more than $395.83/month, you'll qualify.

Calculating the Subsidy

Income	Maximum Premium
<133% (of FPL)	2% (of income)
133 – 150%	3-4%
150 – 200%	4-6.3%
200 – 250%	6.3-8.05%
250 – 300%	8.05-9.5%
300 – 400%	9.5%

The goal of the subsidy is to make sure you don't spend an unreasonably high percentage of your income on health insurance. So in some ways, it won't really matter how much the actual premium costs – if you're eligible for subsidies, you'll only have to spend so much of your income for your coverage.

The subsidies are based on the cost of the second-lowest cost "silver" plan in the state. Your premium will vary according to where you live, of course, but the subsidies are designed to always cap your premium at the given percentage.

Now let's look at some specific examples to see how it all works in practice. We'll take our numbers from the Kaiser Family Foundation report we discussed in the last chapter.

In Ohio Rating Area 11 (Cleveland), there are 10 insurers offering coverage, with 27 bronze plans and 30 silver plans. What do actual premiums look like?

- A single adult, age 25, earning $25,000 per year (218% of the FPL) would pay $196/month for the second-lowest cost silver plan (CareSource's "Just4me" plan). The tax credit would be $52/month, making the net premium after subsidy $144/month. The subsidy takes the cost of coverage from 9.4% down to 6.9% of our single adult's income. The lowest-cost bronze plan premium (Kaiser Foundation's "KP OH Bronze HSA plan, with a $5,000 deductible), after subsidy, would be just $88/month.

- A family of four, headed by two adults age 40, earning $60,000 per year (255% of the FPL), will pay $745/month for the second-lowest cost silver plan. Their tax credit will be $336/month, making the net premium after subsidy a more manageable $409/month. The lowest-cost bronze plan, after subsidy, would be just $194/month.

- A married couple, age 60, earning $30,000 per year (193% of the FPL) would pay a whopping $1,058/month for the second-lowest cost silver plan. However, their tax credit will be $908/month, making the net premium after subsidy a more affordable $150/month. The lowest-cost bronze plan costs $752/month, meaning no out-of-pocket cost after the tax subsidy.

Premiums for similarly-situated consumers will vary by location. However, the subsidies are designed to limit premiums to the given percentage of your income no matter where you live. In California's Rating Area 15 (Los Angeles), for example, our family of four earning $60,000 would pay $763, rather than $745, for their second-lowest cost silver plan. However, their subsidy would be $354/month, bringing the net after-subsidy cost down to the $409/month, just like in Ohio. The same family living in Maryland Rating Area 1 (Baltimore) would face a $683 "rack rate" for their coverage, with a $273 subsidy bringing their net cost down to the same $409 as in Cleveland or Los Angeles.

The subsidy itself takes the form of a "refundable" tax credit. A tax credit is a dollar-for-dollar reduction in your tax bill. Most credits are "nonrefundable," which means if your tax credits are more than your actual tax, you pay no tax and lose the difference. But the insurance subsidy is a "refundable" credit. That means if the subsidy is more than your actual tax, the IRS will send you a check for the difference.

Ordinarily, this would mean filing your tax return for the year you pay for the coverage, then subtracting the subsidy from that year's tax or waiting for the IRS to send you a refund. But most families just don't have the cash flow to wait around for a check. So the good news here is that you can apply for the tax credit when you apply for the insurance, and the government will pay the subsidy directly to the insurance company.

The *bad* news here is that just applying for the subsidy might be a bit of an ordeal. The Department of Health and Human Service's first draft of the "single streamlined application" for subsidies ran 21 pages and asked for about 1,000 separate pieces of information. (The revised version shrank to just three.) Are you eligible for coverage somewhere else, like

Medicaid or Tricare? Is anyone in your household pregnant or disabled? How much do you make from farming or fishing? What coverage is available at work?

In a perfect world, the government will "check your work,' and make sure everything you put on your insurance application matches up with what you report on your taxes. If your income at the end of the year turns out to be more than you said it would be when you applied, you can wind up owing back part of the subsidy. So you'll want to be careful when you apply.

However, this may not be a major concern, at least for the first few years of Obamacare. On July 5, 2013, the Department of Health and Human Services (HHS) heaved up 606 pages of regulations stating, among other things, that they wouldn't try to verify eligibility for individual subsidies, but would instead rely on "self-reporting." The regulations also gave the exchanges "temporarily expanded discretion to accept an attestation of projected annual household income without further verification." HHS promises to develop a "more robust" verification system someday in the future, but they confess it's just not feasible yet.

The Employer Mandate

Employer Requirements

Size	Requirements
Up to 50	• No requirement to provide coverage • Employees may qualify for subsidies on exchange
50+	• Must cover full-timers • Must start coverage 90 days after hire • Subject to "free rider" penalty

You've probably heard that Obamacare requires employers to offer health insurance or face some pretty hefty fines. That's not entirely true. Congress wanted employers to provide coverage. But the law doesn't actually *require* them to provide anything. Instead, it imposes a "backdoor" penalty, called the "free rider" penalty, on certain employers who don't comply with "employer shared responsibility" requirements.

The law doesn't even apply to most employers. If you have 50 or fewer full-time equivalents, there's no requirement to provide coverage at all.

If you have more than 50 employees, then you generally have to cover full-time employees working 30 or more hours per week. You have to start coverage no later than 90 days after they start work. And you'll also be subject to the actual penalty. (Remember, the Obama administration has pushed back the effective date to January 1, 2015.)

Free-Rider Penalty

Employer owes penalty *if*:

- More than 50 FTEs
  and . . .
- One or more employees receives premium subsidies to buy insurance on an exchange

---

This rule has gotten a lot of attention – you've no doubt heard about business owners threatening to cut employee hours or deliberately stay small to avoid these requirements. But is it really such a big deal? Is it really the job killer opponents make it out to be? Well, let's take a look.

First, you have to determine if you're even subject to the requirement. To meet that test, you have to have more than 50 employees or full-time equivalents (FTEs):

- For purposes of this rule, one FTE equals 30 hours of work per week or 130 hours of work per month. (Example: two employees each working 15 hours per week equal one FTE.) The goal here is to prevent you from hiring a ton of part-timers to game the system and avoid the penalties.

- The "controlled group" rules mean that employers with common owners get aggregated together to determine whether they meet the threshold. You can't take one company with 100 employees and break it into two separate companies to sidestep the rule.

Okay, so you have 50 or more FTEs and you're subject to the rule. What has to happen for you to wind up paying the penalty? There are two scenarios that could cost you:

1. You don't offer coverage to at least 90% of your *full-time* employees and their dependents, **and** at least one of your full-time employees receives a subsidy to buy insurance on their appropriate local exchange. (Read that carefully – it means you don't have to cover your employees' spouses.)

   Or ...

2. The coverage you offer your full-time employees is "unaffordable" or doesn't provide "minimum value," **and** at least one of your full-time employees receives the insurance subsidy.

The second part of those scenarios surprises a lot of people. You don't automatically get hit with the penalty just by failing to offer coverage, or even by offering substandard coverage. Someone has to actually go out and actually receive a subsidy to buy insurance on their local exchange before the penalty applies. And that "someone" has to be a full-time employee, not just a part-timer.

Looking at a couple of other definitions, what does "affordable" coverage mean? Coverage is unaffordable if a full-time employee has to pay more than 9.5% of his or her income. If it's not more than 9.5% of his own wages, as reported on form W2, it's automatically deemed "affordable."

What constitutes "minimum value"? The plan must cover, on average, 60% of the plan's total cost of incurred benefits – the equivalent of "bronze" coverage on the state exchange.

Calculating the Penalty

Coverage?	Penalty Calculation
No	$2,000 per employee after first 30
Yes	Lesser of: • $3,000 per subsidized employee • $2,000/employee after first 30

Now let's talk about actually *calculating* that penalty.

If you don't offer any health coverage at all, and you meet the two conditions we just discussed, the penalty is $2,000 per full-time employee, *after* subtracting the first 30 full-timers. So, if you have 51 full-timers and 100 part-timers, and one of the *full*-timers gets a subsidy to buy coverage on their state exchange, your penalty will be $42,000, or $2,000 for each of the 21 *full*-time employees *after* the first 30. The *part*-timers' hours go into calculating whether or not you're subject to the penalty; however, you don't actually owe anything for failing to cover them. Got it?

If you *do* offer some sort of substandard coverage, but one or more employees still qualify for subsidies, the penalty is the *lesser* of: 1) $3,000 for each employee who gets subsidies or 2) $2,000 per employee after the first 30. So, you might actually come out ahead by providing lesser coverage, even if one or more of your employees wind up getting subsidies on the exchange. It all depends on the cost of the coverage you provide. You'll just have to run the numbers and see.

Payments are actually calculated separately for each month in which you fail to provide coverage and based on the number of full-time employees for that particular month (minus the first 30, of course). So, failing the requirement for a month or two doesn't mean you're stuck with the full $2,000 or $3,000 annual penalty.

And just like with the individual mandate, there are some conditions where the penalty doesn't apply:

- You won't owe any penalty for part-time employees, even if they wind up getting subsidies to buy coverage on the local exchange.

- You won't owe the penalty for an employee who declines coverage.

- You won't owe the penalty if an employee gets coverage somewhere other than through the local exchange (such as through a spouse, or retiree benefits from a previous job).

Oh, and just because you'll ask . . . no, that penalty is *not* tax-deductible. So, no, the IRS will *not* be interested in sharing your pain.

So, just how big a deal *is* this penalty? Maybe not as big as you think. Right now, nearly 96% of all companies with 50 or more employees already offer some form of health benefits to their employees. That's 5.8 million out of approximately 6 million total firms. So we're really talking about a very small number of potential penalties. And many of those firms that don't already offer coverage will find themselves better equipped to do so, either because of lower costs in general or wider choices through the health insurance exchanges.

Options for Individuals

- Do nothing
- Keep current plan
- Turn to exchange
- MERP
- Health Savings Accounts

Now that we've looked at the new rules, let's tie it all together. What are your options if you're out there shopping for health insurance for yourself?

Your first option is to simply do . . . nothing. If you're comfortable taking the risk of living without insurance, there's nothing that says you have to go out and buy it. You'll owe a tax penalty starting in 2014. But as we already discussed, the IRS has no statutory authority to enforce that penalty. It may turn out that all the controversy over the "individual mandate" amounts to nothing.

If you already have coverage, and you're happy with it, you can keep it. No need to worry about exchanges, or minimum coverages, or free rider penalties, or anything else. Of course, your premiums will probably keep going up year after year, just like they do now.

If you already have coverage and you're *not* happy with it, you can scrap it. You may find it's cheaper and easier to buy through one of the new exchanges. But now you'll have a way to compare coverage and benefits on an apples-to-apples basis, with more information than you had before.

You might also want to consider taking advantage of a Section 105 Medical Expense Reimbursement Plan, Health Savings Account (HSA), or Flexible Spending Account (FSA) for help with out-of-pocket costs. We'll talk about those next.

Medical Expense Reimbursement Plan

MERP/105 Plan

- *Employee* benefit plan
  - Married: Hire spouse (no salary necessary)
  - Not married: C-corp
- Reimburse employee for medical expenses incurred for self, spouse, and dependents
- Works with any insurance
  - Choose your own
  - Supplement spouse's coverage

Obamacare focuses mainly on helping Americans afford insurance. But insurance rarely covers the cost of everything. Most of us still face out-of-pocket deductibles, co-pays, co-insurance, and other costs. What options do we have to help minimize those costs?

One way to lower your costs is to make your healthcare expenses tax-deductible. If you pay for your own health insurance, and you're self-employed, you can deduct your premium as an adjustment to income on Page 1 of Form 1040. If you're not self-employed, you can still deduct your premium, along with the rest of your out-of-pocket costs, on Schedule A. But in both cases, that deduction only counts if it's more than 10% of your adjusted gross income. And most of us just don't spend that much of our income on healthcare. So we wind up with no real deduction.

If you're self-employed, there might be a way to write off your insurance premiums, along with your out-of-pocket costs, as a *business* expense. It's called a Medical Expense Reimbursement Plan, or Section 105 Plan.

This is an employee benefit plan, which means (spoiler alert) it requires an employee. If your business is taxed as a "C" corporation, you qualify as your own employee, so you can simply hire yourself. But if your business is taxed as a sole proprietorship, partnership, or "S" corporation, you're considered self-employed. So, if you're married, hire your spouse. You don't even have to pay him or her a salary. You can compensate your spouse in the form of benefits only, which avoids the hassle of filing payroll returns. The only requirement here is that the benefits you pay have to be "reasonable compensation" for the service they perform. If your spouse works an hour a month filing invoices for you, you'll probably have a hard time convincing an auditor that

that's "reasonable compensation" for $4,000 worth of LASIK surgery!

The main exception to the hire-your-spouse rule is the "S" corporation. If you own more than 2% of the stock, you and your spouse are both considered self-employed for purposes of this rule. You'll need to use another source of income, not taxed as an "S" corporation, as the basis for this plan. (Alternatively, you might consider setting up a Health Savings Account, which we'll discuss shortly.)

Eligible Expenses

- Major medical, LTC, Medicare, "Medigap"
- Co-pays, deductibles, prescriptions
- Dental, vision, and chiropractic
- Braces, fertility treatments, special schools
- Nonprescription medications and supplies

Once the plan is in place, you can reimburse your employee for any medical expense they incur for themselves, their spouse, and their dependents.

- This includes any kind of health insurance, including major medical, long-term care (up to specific IRS limits),

Medicare premiums, and even Medigap coverage.

- It includes all your copays, deductibles, "co-insurance,' and other amounts insurance doesn't pay.

- It includes all your prescription drugs.

- It includes expenses for things like dental care, vision care, and chiropractic care that traditional insurance might not cover.

- It includes some really "big-ticket" items like braces for your kids' teeth, fertility treatments, and special schools for learning-disabled children. Let's say your physician diagnoses your 8-year-old son with ADHD, and prescribes *tai kwon do* lessons. Guess what – those lessons are now tax-deductible!

- It even includes over-the-counter medications and supplies, so long as they're actually prescribed by a physician.

One big advantage of the MERP is that it works with any insurance policy. You don't have to buy special coverage. You can use a MERP with insurance you buy on your own or insurance you buy through an exchange. If your spouse gets coverage from their employer, you can even set up a MERP in your business to cover whatever out-of-pocket expenses your spouse's insurance doesn't cover.

Let's assume you're a sole proprietor with two kids and you've hired your husband to work for your business. The plan lets you reimburse your husband/employee for all medical and dental expenses he incurs for himself – his spouse (which brings you into the plan) – and his dependents, the kids.

This includes all the expenses listed above.

The best part is, this is money you'd spend anyway, whether you get a deduction or not. You'll spend your money on glasses or your kids' braces whether it's deductible or not. The MERP just lets you move it from someplace on your return where you certainly can't deduct all of it (and probably can't deduct *any* of it), to a place where you can.

MERP Requirements

- Written plan document
- No pre-funding required
  - Reimburse employee
  - Pay provider directly
- Bypass 10% floor
- Minimize self-employment tax

Okay, how do you make it work? Well, you'll need a written plan document. You'll need to track your expenses under the plan. And you'll report reimbursements as "employee benefits" on Schedule C, Form 1065, or Form 1120. You'll save income tax *and* self-employment tax.

There's no pre-funding required. You don't have to open a special bank or investment account, like with Health Savings

Accounts or flex-spending plans. You don't have to decide up front how much you want to contribute to the plan, like you do with flexible spending accounts, and there's no "use it or lose it" rule. The MERP is really just an accounting device that lets you recharacterize your family medical bills as a business expense.

Here's one important requirement that the IRS *will* pay attention to in the unlikely event you get audited. You *do* have to run the payments through the actual business. You can't just pay medical bills out of the family personal account, total them up at the end of the year, and throw them on the business return.

This means you have two choices. You can pay health-care providers directly out of the business account. Or you can reimburse your employees for expenses they pay out of their personal funds. Let's say your husband needs to pick up a prescription. He can use his own money, and you can reimburse him. Or he can use a business credit card and charge it to the business directly.

The MERP doesn't just help you save *income* tax. It also helps you save *self-employment* tax. Remember, when you work for yourself, you pay a special self-employment tax, which replaces the Social Security and Medicare taxes that you and your employer would share on your salary. That self-employment tax is based on your "net self-employment earnings." And when you set up a MERP, the deduction reduces that self-employment income.

MERP Requirements

- Must cover "eligible employees"
- Exclusions
    - Under age 25
    - Under 35 hours/week
    - Under 9 months/year
    - Under 3 years service
    - Collective bargaining agreement
- Excise tax on Form 720

Now, here's the bad news. If you have non-family employees, you have to include them too. Now, you can exclude employees under age 25, who work less than 35 hours per week, less than nine months per year, or who have worked for you less than three years. You can also exclude employees covered by a collective bargaining agreement that includes health benefits. But still, having non-family employees may make it too expensive to reimburse everyone as generously as you'd cover your own family.

Obamacare also imposes a pesky new excise tax requirement on MERPs called the "Patient Centered Outcomes Research Trust Fund Fee," or PCORI fee. For plans operating in 2012, that meant a $1 per person tax, reported on IRS Form 720, and due by July 31.

Yes, you heard that right. One buck. Eight bits. You can't even buy a pack of gum for that much. But the statutory penalty for failing to file that report can be as high as $10,000. And while it's not likely the IRS will ever actually impose that fine, you still want to make sure you dot your "i's" and cross your "t's."

And don't laugh at that one-dollar fee. For plans operating in 2013 or later, it doubles – all the way up to *$2* per person! (Oh, and don't be surprised if it doubles a few *more* times in the future!)

Health Savings Accounts

Health Savings Accounts

1. "High deductible health plan"
   - $1,250+ deductible (individual coverage)
   - $2,500+ deductible (family coverage)

Plus

2. Tax-deductible "Health Savings Account"
   - Contribute & deduct up to $3,250/$6,450 per year
   - Account grows tax-free
   - Tax-free withdrawals for qualified expenses

If a medical expense reimbursement plan isn't appropriate – either because you don't have a spouse to hire, or you have non-family employees you would have to cover – consider establishing a Health Savings Account. These arrangements combine a high-deductible health plan with a tax-free savings account to cover unreimbursed costs.

To qualify, you'll need to be covered by a "high deductible health plan." This means the deductible is at least $1,250 for single coverage or $2,500 for family coverage. Neither you nor your spouse can be covered by a "*non*-high deductible health plan" or Medicare. The plan can't cover any expense, other than certain preventive care benefits, until you satisfy the annual deductible. You're not eligible if you're covered by a separate plan or rider offering prescription drug benefits before the minimum annual deductible is satisfied.

Once you've established your eligibility, you can open a deductible "health savings account" to cover out-of-pocket expenses not covered by your insurance. For 2013, you can contribute up to $3,250 if you have individual coverage or $6,450 if you have family coverage. (If you're 55 or older, you can save an extra $1,000 per year.)

HSAs are easy to open. Most banks, brokerage firms, and insurance companies offer them. Many times you can even get a debit card to charge expenses directly to the account.

Once you're up and running, you can use your account for most kinds of health insurance, including COBRA continuation and long-term care (but not "Medigap" coverage). You can also use it for the same sort of expenses as a MERP – copays, deductibles, prescriptions, and other out-of-pocket costs.

Withdrawals are tax-free so long as you use them for "qualified medical costs." Withdrawals *not* used for qualified medical costs are subject to regular income tax plus a 20% penalty.

After your death, your account passes to your specified beneficiary. If your beneficiary is your spouse, they can treat it as their own HSA. If not, your beneficiary will pay ordinary tax on the account proceeds (but not the 20% penalty).

The Health Savings Account isn't quite as powerful or flexible as the MERP. You've got specific dollar limits on what you can contribute to the account, which might not match your out-of-pocket costs. And there's no self-employment tax advantage as there is with a MERP. But Health Savings Accounts can still help cut your overall health-care costs by giving you bigger tax deductions.

Flexible Spending Accounts

Flexible spending accounts ("FSAs") let you set aside pre-tax dollars for a variety of nontaxable fringe benefits, including health and disability insurance and medical expense reimbursement. (Some employers also offer FSAs for daycare costs, but we'll skip those in the interest of sticking to Obamacare.) Plan contributions avoid federal income and FICA tax.

The new rules let you contribute up to $2,500 per year to your account. Before Obamacare, there were no contribution limits at all. Many observers have called the new $2,500 limit a tax in disguise, especially for older workers with expensive prescriptions who tend to contribute more to their accounts.

Once the money is in the account, you can use it for most medical expenses. However, nonprescription drugs and supplies, long-term care coverage associated and expenses are not eligible FSA expenses.

Your employer deducts plan contributions from your paycheck and deposits them into your account until you claim your reimbursements.

When you enroll, you have to choose how much to contribute each pay period. You generally can't change your contribution amount in the middle of the plan year unless there's a change in your "family status." Eligible changes include marriage or divorce; birth, adoption, or death of a child; spousal employment; change in a dependent's student status; and the like.

You can claim your full year's reimbursement as soon as you incur qualifying expenses, whether you've fully funded your account for that amount or not.

Historically, FSA rules have required you to use your account balance by the end of the year or forfeit it. However, many employers' plans have taken advantage of a subsequent ruling that lets them amend their plans to provide a 2½ month grace period immediately following the end of the year.

Options for Small Employers

Options for Employers (<51)

- Do nothing
- Keep current plan
- Cut employees loose
- Consider Medicaid/CHIP plans

Now that we've looked at options for individuals, what are your options if you're an employer? We'll start by discussing your options if you have 50 or fewer employees.

Your first option is to simply do . . . nothing. That may be what you're already doing, and if it's working for you, that's fine. If your employees are content buying their own insurance on the private market, or relying on their spouses' coverage, or even going without coverage, that's fine. In fact, they might even be delighted when they see all the new choices and new subsidies available starting in 2014. Most employees don't know anything about buying health insurance, for the simple reason that they've never had to do it. But they might be surprised, starting next year, to find that a little education goes a long way.

The problem with doing nothing, of course, is that in most industries, as employers get bigger, your employees come to expect some sort of health plan. Why? Well, it's really just a historical accident dating back to World War II. During the war, wage and price controls limited how much employers could pay their employees. To get around those rules, employers started offering healthcare benefits in addition to salary, and that led to our current employer-based healthcare system. But in the end, it doesn't matter *why* employees expect you to offer healthcare coverage. It just matters that they *do* expect it.

If you currently offer your employees group health insurance, and the plan you have is working for you, you can keep it. No need to worry about exchanges, or minimum coverages, or free rider penalties. Of course, your premiums will probably keep going up year after year, just like they do now. And if you require your employees to pay part of their premium, don't be surprised if some of them hop off your plan and join an exchange plan. That's fine – you won't have to worry about paying for the cost of their claims anymore, and there won't be any legal consequences for their decision. (Of course, if your plan "participation" drops below a certain level, your current insurance company may drop your coverage. But that's a different problem.)

If you already have a plan, and you're not happy with it, you can scrap it. You may find it's cheaper and easier to cut your employees loose and let them find coverage on their own. You can still cover part or all of their premium and out-of-pocket costs. You'll just do it with a Section 105 plan instead of a group insurance policy.

Let's take a step back here and look at the big picture. There are thousands of employers across the country who understand their employees expect them to provide health benefits. But those employers don't want to take on the risk of big claims. So they transfer that risk to an insurance company. That's the whole point of insurance, after all.

So they go out and buy a group insurance policy. And now they find they're in the group insurance business. They're stuck deciding what benefits to offer their employees, choosing coverage from a confusing selection of contracts, guesstimating how much they'll wind up paying for higher premiums every year, and even dealing with teed-off employees when an insurance reimbursement gets stuck in red tape and a doctor sends a bill to collections.

They're stuck. They know they need to keep offering quality benefits to attract and retain employees. Obamacare doesn't change that. But they don't want the headache of maintaining a group health insurance policy.

Here's our recommendation. We look at the traditional employer-based benefits model, which uses tax exclusions to help make health insurance more affordable, and compare it to the new Obamacare model, which uses subsidies to make individual insurance more affordable. Which cost reduction tool is more generous, the tax break or the subsidy? For most employees, the subsidies will be more valuable moving forward. So we recommend you consider this strategy:

1. Drop your group health plan entirely. Just get rid of it. (Go ahead, take a minute to hyperventilate. We know this is a big step. But trust us, you'll probably like it. Remember the first time you got behind the wheel of a car? That was

scary, too.)

2. Let your employees go out and choose their own coverage on the exchange. They'll probably be happier in the long run taking charge of their own coverage. And they may even find it for less than what they're paying now for the coverage you've picked for them.

3. Set up a Section 125 "premium only" plan, also called a POP plan, to deduct their premium from their paycheck. You're probably already using something like this right now for your current group insurance.

4. Set up a Section 105 Medical Expense Reimbursement Plan to cover the difference between the coverage your employees get now on the exchange and what they would have gotten from your old plan. You can design it specifically to cover the difference between, say, a "silver" level plan and your old plan.

You'll save thousands starting in the very first month, at no cost to your employees.

That last step, by the way, is where *we* come in – we'll design and administer that plan for you, for a surprisingly reasonable fee. And there you'll have done it. You'll be among the first of a wave of companies taking advantage of Obamacare to give your employees the benefits they deserve, without letting group insurance premiums squeeze your bottom line.

If your employees are generally lower paid, so that they qualify for subsidies and don't get much value from the tax exclusion, they'll probably come out ahead with the exchange. If they're higher paid, so that they don't qualify for the subsidy but get greater value from the tax exclusion, there may be less advantage. The only way to find out is to compare.

Medicaid/CHIP Plans

Medicaid/CHIP

- Medicaid available up to 138% of FPL
- CHIP coverage typically available up to 200% of FPL
- Coverage is free to employees

Your lower-paid employees might want to consider taking advantage of Medicaid and "CHIP" programs, rather than commercial insurance, to cut their own costs. So now let's talk about how that might work.

Medicaid and state Childrens' Health Insurance Plans, or "CHIP" plans, are currently the main source of healthcare coverage for lower income working families. But the new Obamacare rules let employers take advantage of those programs to help finance coverage for their employees.

- Employees are eligible for Medicaid if they're under age 65 and their income is below 138% of the federal poverty level (FPL). In 2013, that means $15,856 for an individual or $32,499 for a family of four.

- Typically, children are eligible for state CHIP programs if their family income is below 200% of the FPL.

Why would an employee choose to go on Medicaid or a CHIP program? Well, because it's free. And it stretches their healthcare dollar if they don't have to use it for basic coverage.

Let's say you're a business owner and you've terminated your group health plan. You have an employee with a child who makes $24,000 per year. She can certainly go out and buy coverage on her state exchange. But even after getting a subsidy, she'll probably pay at least *some* premium. And she'll still have out-of-pocket expenses to cover for herself and her child.

Or, she could enroll in Medicaid and enroll her child in the CHIP program. Now she'll get all her basic coverage that probably still would have cost her at least something for free. Now she can use any employer reimbursement for the inevitable out-of-pocket expenses that even the insurance she buys on the exchange wouldn't have covered.

Options for Larger Employers

Options for Employers (51+)

- Do nothing
- Keep current plan
- Modify current plan

Finally, what are the options for employers with more than 50 employees? Remember, these rules don't kick in until 2015. But it's still important to understand them now so you can anticipate your future moves.

Your first option, again, is to simply do . . . nothing. If you don't currently have a plan, doing nothing and paying the penalty may actually be cheaper than establishing your own plan. Your employees may resent you for it – but that's your decision to make. And if you do nothing, your employees can still find coverage on their own through the local exchange. They may even be happier with the coverage they find on their own than with the coverage you could afford to buy them. There probably won't be any shortage of big employers who grumble and pay the penalty rather than offer a benefit they just can't afford.

If you already offer your employees a plan, you can keep it if it's good enough to protect you from the penalty. Or you can modify it to protect yourself if it's not. To protect yourself, you need to make sure your plan meets two requirements. These are the "safe harbors" that will protect you from the free rider penalty:

- You have to offer your employees "qualified coverage." That means the benefit has to be equivalent at least to the "bronze" level coverage they would get from your local insurance exchange.

- You have to make sure your employees don't pay more than 9.5% of their income towards their premium. So, for example, if your lowest-paid employee makes $20,000 per year, and your required monthly employee contribution is $158.33 or less, you're safe.

If you meet both of those requirements, you'll avoid the penalty. Even if an employee buys coverage through an exchange, they won't qualify for *subsidies* – and remember, the penalty isn't triggered until an employee gets *subsidies* to buy coverage on an exchange.

It's worth mentioning that, starting in 2014, businesses with up to 100 employees are welcome to buy coverage on the local "Small Business Health Options Program," or SHOP exchange. Beginning in 2016, states can choose to allow larger employers to participate as well.

Options for Self-Insured Plans

- Cover costs directly
- Buy stop-loss to limit risk
- Use Obamacare to cut risk

Many companies above a certain size – typically 500 or more employees – choose to "self-insure" their employees, or "self-fund" their plans. That is, they look to save money by cutting out the insurance company middleman and pay benefits and claims directly out of their own pocket. There's usually at least *some* insurance involved – typically, self-funded plans still buy a "stop-loss" policy to limit their risk to, say, $50,000 or $100,000 per employee in case of really big claims like cancers or birth defects. And self-insured plans usually "rent" an insurance company's network to administer the paperwork and manage claims on behalf of employees. But the concept here is pretty straightforward – why not save money when your size makes it cheaper to take the risk yourself than pay an insurance company to take it for you?

Self-insured plans are subject to most of the "big" Obamacare changes like pre-existing conditions, dependent coverage, coverage limits, and waiting periods. However, many plans are "grandfathered" so they can continue operating essentially as before Obamacare. If you're subject to a collective bargaining agreement, for example, you can continue operating the plan until the date on which the last agreement relating to the plan expires.

But self-insured employers can still benefit from Obamacare by using the new rules to lower their risk of claims. And that's an important benefit.

Let's say you run a manufacturing company with 500 employees. You've chosen to self-insure up to $100,000 per employee. That leaves you with a theoretical risk of up to $50 million in claims. Now, we know not everyone will cost that much. But you might still have, say, six employees, spouses, or dependents with cancers, birth defects, or other expensive conditions costing $100,000 in a year. Plus you'll have all the rest of your 500 employees' claims.

Why not cut those six employees loose from your own plan, send them to their local exchange (where they can't be denied coverage for those preexisting conditions), and set up a Medical Expense Reimbursement Plan to cover the difference between the benefits they get from the exchange and the benefits they enjoyed under your self-insured plan? You can even "bribe" them, if you like, by bumping up their salary to cover the cost of their coverage on the exchange.

That would send $600,000 (minus the cost of buying their coverage on the exchange) straight to your own bottom line. As long as they don't qualify for subsidies, you'll be safe from the free-rider penalty.

In fact – if the numbers work – why not cut *all* of your employees loose from your self-funded group plan, and send them *all* out on their own? Now you'll eliminate your risk, and save even more when you don't have to hire an HR staff to manage the plan.

Yes, this is "unfair." In insurance terminology, it's a perfect example of "adverse selection," technically defined as a situation where an individual's demand for insurance goes up with the insured's risk of loss, and the insurer is unable to compensate by charging higher premiums. It's certainly not what the authors of Obamacare intended when they wrote the law. But many businesses will see this as an opportunity to eliminate significant risks that can jeopardize coverage for everyone. And isn't that part of the reason for Obamacare in the first place?

If you feel guilty asking employees to go out and choose their own coverage, you can keep a staffer or two on hand to help them make sense of the coverage. (They can play the same role as the "navigators" we discussed on the insurance exchanges.) But again, you might find your employees would *rather* find their own coverage than settle for whatever doctors, hospitals, pharmacies, and benefits *you* pick *for* them. If you run a manufacturing company, you might legitimately decide your efforts are best spent in the *manufacturing* business and not the benefits management business.

Medicare Tax On Income

- 0.9% surtax
- $200,000+ for individuals
- $250,000 for joint filers

Now let's talk about some new taxes we all face under the Obamacare rules, whether we're healthy or not. Specifically, We're talking about the new Medicare surtax and "unearned income Medicare contribution" rules. These aren't tied to any specific benefit under the law. They're just designed to raise general revenue to help pay for the new law.

You already pay a Medicare tax on all of your "earned income" from salaries and wages and business income:

- If you're paid as an employee, your employer pays an amount equal to 1.45% of your gross earnings (including anything you contribute to a retirement account) and withholds another 1.45% directly from your pay.

- If you're self-employed, you pay a self-employment tax of 2.9% on your "net self employment income." This represents both "halves" that you and your employer would pay if you weren't self-employed.

Obamacare adds a 0.9% surtax, on top of the current 2.9%, on earned income above $200,000 for individuals and $250,000 for joint filers. 0.9% may not sound like a lot. But it's still $900 in new tax for every extra hundred thousand dollars in income. It'll add up fast. And there's really not much you can do other than *not* earn the income.

If you're self-employed, you might consider restructuring part of your business to recharacterize some of your profits as "passive" income. Such a move would eliminate the current 2.9% tax on that income and avoid the 0.9% surtax. However, depending on how you earn your income and how your business is structured, that may not always be a realistic option.

Medicare Tax on Investments

Medicare Tax on Investments

- 3.8% tax
- Individuals >$200k
- Joint filers >$250k

"Investment Income"
- Interest
- Dividends
- Capital gains
- Rents
- Royalties
- Annuities

There's also a new 3.8% "unearned income Medicare contribution" on investment income. (Doesn't "unearned income Medicare contribution" sound so much better than "tax"? Aren't you going to be so much happier paying an "unearned income Medicare contribution" than you would be paying another "tax"?)

The new tax applies on "net investment income," which the law defines to include interest, dividends, capital gains, rents, royalties, and taxable withdrawals from annuities. It kicks in at the same levels as the Medicare surtax -- $200,000 for individuals and $250,000 for joint filers. So, for example, if you file singly, and you have $210,000 of earned income plus $10,000 of investment income, you'll pay the 0.9% surtax on

your last $10,000 of earned income and the 3.8% tax on
$10,000 of investment income.

Avoid Medicare Tax

- Choose tax-efficient investments
- Match gains and losses

Avoiding at least some of the 3.8% unearned income Medicare
contribution may not be as hard as you think. It's really a
matter of choosing tax-efficient investments. The same
strategies that help you pay less regular tax on your investment
income will also help you avoid the Medicare tax.

Your first line of defense is choosing investments that don't
generate taxable income. If you're investing for income, for
example, bank account interest and most bond interest is fully
taxable. That means they're subject to regular tax, plus the new
Medicare tax. But municipal bonds are free from federal and
most state tax income. So shifting fixed-income portions of
your overall portfolio will help defeat the Medicare tax.

If you're investing for retirement, you can choose to wrap your investments in tax-deferred wrappers like IRAs, Roth IRAs, and qualified retirement plans, which will shelter their income from regular tax as well as the new Medicare tax.

Avoiding the new tax on capital gains may be harder. If circumstances make *now* the right time to sell an appreciated asset – whether it's a stock, mutual fund, real estate, or even your business – then you shouldn't let the tax consequence scare you out of making the right investment move. But you might look at strategies like matching capital gains and losses to at least trim the effect of making the right investment move. For example, if it's time to sell a stock, and you've got a $10,000 gain, is there another stock with a $10,000 *loss* you can sell to offset that gain?

Home Sales: Rumor vs. Reality

Rumor	Reality
• $475,000 sale	• $475,000 sale
X 3.8% tax rate	- $125,000 "basis"
= $ 18,050 tax	- $ 50,000 improvements
	- $250,000 exclusion
	= $ 50,000 gain
	X 3.8% tax rate
	= $ 1,900 tax

There's one especially irresponsible rumor going around about this new tax that we want to address head-on. Specifically, we're talking about the rumor that Obamacare imposes a 3.8% tax on selling your house.

Let's say you're single and you bought your home 20 years ago for $125,000. You've added $50,000 in improvements, and now you're selling it for $475,000 after commissions, closing costs, and other expenses.

If the rumor is correct, when you walk away from the closing with your cash, you'll owe Uncle Sam 3.8% of that amount, or $18,050.

That may make for exciting rants on talk radio. But the reality is a lot less harsh. You may owe a tax. But it won't be on the full $475,000. You'll just *start* with that amount. Then you'll subtract your original "basis" in the house – in this case, the $125,000 you paid 20 years ago. Then you'll subtract the $50,000 you paid in improvements. That leaves you with a $300,000 gain. But then you'll subtract your Section 121 exclusion – in this case, $250,000. (If you were married filing jointly, that exclusion would be $500,000). That leaves you with a $50,000 gain. If your other income, added to the gain, puts you above the $200,000 threshold, you'll owe the Medicare tax. But even then, the tax on the home sale portion will be 3.8% of the $50,000 gain, or $1,900.

We're not here to tell you that paying a $1,900 tax on your gain will be fun. But it's a lot easier than paying the rumored 3.8% on the full $475,000 sale price!

Red Tape Alert!

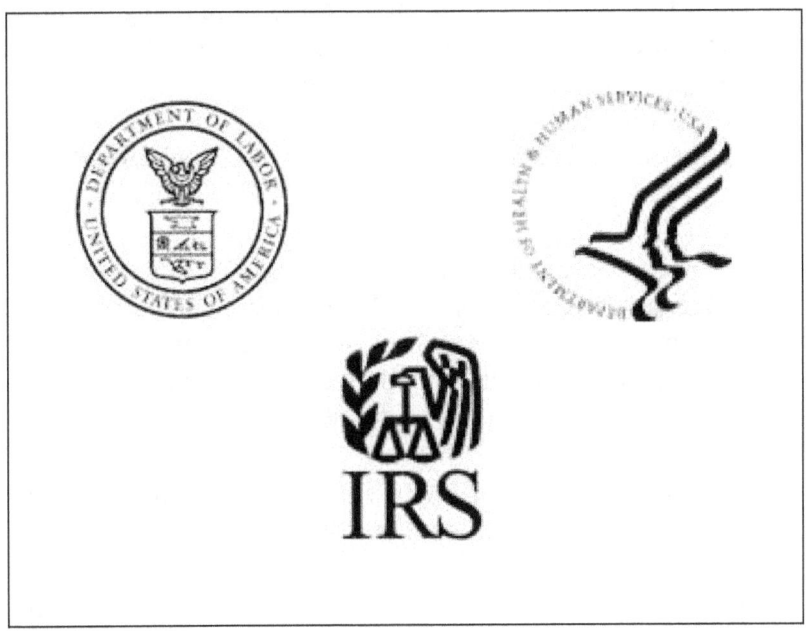

Now that we've talked about the specific provisions of the new law, let's touch on how it's all going to work.

If you like government red tape, you'll love Obamacare. The law has over 500 specific provisions, with almost 50 major changes to the Tax Code. The Treasury Inspector General for Tax Administration says "Tax provisions included in the Affordable Care Act represent the largest set of tax law changes the IRS has had to implement in more than 20 years."

The actual text of the two bills that make up Obamacare run over 2,500 pages. Future regulations will run tens of thousands more pages – for example, on February 20, 2013, the Department of Health and Human Services released a final rule establishing "minimum essential health benefits" for plans sold by the new insurance exchanges that ran 149 pages all by itself. On July 5, they heaved up another 606-page rule governing applications for premium subsidies. So, for most of us at least, this isn't going to be an easy process.

As for enforcement, there will be lots of people with their fingers in the pie. But three agencies will be most important:

- The Department of Health and Human Services will be primarily responsible for the insurance and benefits provisions of the law. They'll issue regulations, promulgate standards, and generally do the sort of things you'd expect HHS to do with a law this vast.

- The Department of Labor will focus on regulating how employers deliver benefits to employees.

- The IRS will be primarily responsible for the financial provisions. They'll collect information from employers and insurance companies, figure out who qualifies for subsidies and Medicaid coverage, determine who owes penalties, and penalize employers who don't play ball. The IRS has already created *eight* new offices, with over 2,100 employees, to enforce the law. And the Obama administration has requested $440 million in new funding to *pay* for it all.

That's a LOT of work for all three agencies. It's probably not being cynical to say we should expect a fair amount of hiccups along the way!

Continuing Challenges to Obamacare

Continuing Challenges

- Repeal efforts
- State challenges/nullification
- Congressional nullification

You would think that three years after passage, Obamacare opponents would move on to new fights. Well, you would be wrong. The opposition isn't folding, even though the Supreme Court has upheld the law as constitutional.

Many congressional Republicans continue to vow to overturn Obamacare, in full. They don't have the votes to do it – at least not in the Senate – and they certainly aren't going to get the support they would need to override a Presidential veto even if they *do* overturn it. But opponents, especially in the House of Representatives, still have enough clout to make political hay. In fact, on May 15, 2013, the House voted for the 37th *time* to repeal Obamacare, just to give 70 first-term representatives *their* first chance to go on record as opposing the law. And that was hardly their last effort – as of this writing, they were up to 40 votes for repeal.

State governments have also stepped up to oppose the new law. Many states have objected that it pushes too many costs onto them, especially increased Medicaid costs. Politicians in a majority of states have at least introduced legislation that would limit or oppose various provisions of the law. One state representative in South Carolina introduced legislation that would throw federal officials in jail for trying to enforce Obamacare! You can scoff at seemingly frivolous efforts like that if you like – but even after the Supreme Court's decision to uphold the law, determined opponents can still slow down the process with red tape and court challenges.

Opponents are also attacking specific pieces of the law by refusing to appropriate funds to enforce them. For example, they've introduced legislation blocking funding for the state insurance exchanges, or appropriations for the IRS to enforce the law. These "backdoor" attacks may not achieve the goal of sweeping repeal. But they can still throw a wrench in enforcement just the same. The 2013 IRS scandal over targeting "tea party" organizations for extra scrutiny didn't help matters – several Representatives seized on the scandal to object to expanding IRS authority.

Where Do We Go From Here?

What Does It All Mean?

- Track developments
- Get the right advice

So – where do we go from here?

There's no doubt that what we've seen is just the tip of a whole new iceberg. The way that we Americans pay for healthcare is changing.

You may think it's a good thing, or you may think it's a bad thing. You may think Obamacare is a godsend, or you may think it's a slow-motion trainwreck. But Obamacare is the law of the land. Both houses of Congress passed it. The President signed it. And the Supreme Court upheld it. So, despite the best efforts of political opponents trying to repeal it, it's almost certainly here to stay. So let's make sure we all pay attention to the rules as they develop!

We also want to point out how important it is to get the right advice about all of these changes. None of us knows everything about Obamacare. Don't be afraid to ask *all* your insurance and financial advisors for help. Understand that they may have different perspectives and experiences that can help you make the right choice for *you*.

Be especially careful before you take advice from someone with a financial interest in your decision. If you're a business owner, you may think a "benefits consultant" is the right place to go for answers. But most so-called "benefits consultants" don't actually consult at all – they sell group health insurance! And their compensation can be tied directly to how much you pay. They may say their *commissions* are capped at a specific dollar amount regardless of how much you spend. And that may be true. But they often receive bonuses and overrides that can be more than the commissions themselves. So, for example, they're not likely to share our recommendation on Page 51 that you actually *drop* your group coverage!

Please, call us with your questions. Come to us for a *plan*. If we can't answer you right away, we'll find the answer for you. Just don't panic over changes like the individual mandate or tax on "Cadillac plans." We've got lots of time to see how healthcare reform *really* shakes out.

www.ingramcontent.com/pod-product-compliance
Lightning Source LLC
Chambersburg PA
CBHW071617170526
45166CB00003B/1098